Hist

My Time as a De

the Newberry National Volcanic Monument

Evelyn L. Findley

"Learn from yesterday, live for today, hope for tomorrow. The important thing is not to stop questioning."

Albert Einstein (1879-1955)

Table of Contents

Print ISBN 978-1-938586-40-8
eBook ISBN 978-1-938586-41-5
All Rights Reserved
Copyright © 2013 by Evelyn Findley

Full Color Paperback Edition November 2013
Printed in the United States of America
Writers Cramp Publishing
http://www.writerscramp.us/
editor@writerscramp.us

This is a personal but factual account. All characters, places or events portrayed in this book are accurate to the best of the authors knowledge.

Introduction

We were sitting in Paul's car, up high enough to watch the airplanes come and go at the airport. It was dark, and the lights of Portland were beautiful. The stars were very romantic. I looked at Paul, hoping he was as smitten with me, as I was with him. We were holding hands. I smiled. Then he said, "You know, there's something I don't like about you." Oh, no, my heart sank because I really wanted him to like me. "It's your last name," he added. "Will I ever get a chance to change it?" Was that a proposal? I think I just giggled at first. And that's the way it was with Paul, you never knew what he would come up with next.

I knew when I said yes to his proposal up on Rocky Butte in Portland, Oregon, back in 1954, that life with him would be fun. It would be full of challenging new adventures, lots of laughter and half crazy jokes. When true love comes you never question it. I have heard that you know its true love if you are more concerned with your partners needs than your own. We were engaged about nine months, and were married the following spring, 1955. We started off our marriage in Paul's usually interesting lifestyle of adventure by spending our honeymoon summer, being Forest Fire Look- Outs on Huckleberry Mountain in the Gifford Pinchott National Forest across the Columbia River from Portland in Washington state. It was a perfect honeymoon. We had to leave our car parked at the foot of the mountain and hike up the last three and a half miles with backpacks. The Forest Service took the rest of our stuff up on mules breaking the snow trails right after the 4th of July that year. And we were alone, as we had very little company the whole summer.

My childhood dream was to travel and the desire to be creative. I was not by nature very brave nor self-confident but with Paul I felt complete. I knew he was wise, honest, thoughtful. I trusted him totally and still do.

This is Paul standing by Huckleberry Lookout

I cooked out of cans a lot that summer up on the mountain, and I baked all my own bread on a wood stove. We ate a lot of soup, stew and sandwiches. While Paul dreamed of a new telescope, or a new camera or a microscope, I was dreaming about just having a normal home life someday with some furniture and dishes and things, making a real home. It all came true eventually.

We called ourselves *The Huckleberry Findleys*. Looking back, I can't believe how brave I had to be. When it came time for Paul to enroll for his next year in college, he hiked down and I stayed at the lookout. Later I had to hike down those three and a half miles to the car by myself, flag a log truck driver for a jump start, drive into Portland and find us an apartment and get our stuff moved in. And it seems that first summer of 1955 was just the beginning of our greatly challenging adventure together.

It was absolutely a great experience out in nature's beauty, with a 360 degree view. We could see several snow cap mountains, watch the deer early mornings, and pick wild huckleberries down the hill.

I am standing to the left of the Lookout watching an Eagle that kept wanting to get our kittens. As long as the snow lasted we could melt it for washing and cleaning. The bears came to the snow, but never came any closer. Paul had to carry drinking water uphill 3/4 of a mile, from a spring. He had a tank backpack. We did see lots of deer. The wildflowers were so pretty up there.

So, that was our first time to work for the US Forest Service. And it would be 36 years, 1991, before we worked for them again.

Our second job with the Forest Service lasted for twelve summers, after Paul had taught Science in the public schools for thirty one years, and we had raised three wonderful children. We spent the early part of our retirement being snowbirds to the Southwest in winter and coming back to Oregon to work in summers. *So, in this book, I want to share with you our experiences during our second exciting time working for the US Forest Service in the Newberry National Volcanic Monument, south of Bend, Oregon.*

The main focus of our displays was to share what the evidence tells us about the findings in the Archaeological Digs within the Newberry Caldera and in caves and rock shelters in Central Oregon.

As I write this, Paul and I are celebrating our 58th Wedding Anniversary, and still finding lots of enjoyment in life. A few years ago, we gave up work and moved back to Eugene, Oregon, to be close to our family: three children, four grandsons, and two great grandsons. A lot of my time now is taken up with one small white doggie named *Molly*. Paul has a large garden that keeps him busy, and we have a wealth of friends and family that fills both our lives making them rich and rewarding.

Our Molly is an 8 year old poodle mix. She is a real people lover, and wants to be involved in everything we do. We didn't get her until we retired from snowbirding south and settled down in Eugene, Oregon, in the summer of 2005.

I want to give special thanks to family and friends for reading my manuscript and giving me very constructive suggestions. Thanks to family and friends who gave me permission to use pictures which include them. Thanks to my editor and publisher for his patience. And thanks to my wonderful husband, Paul, for his expertise and support.

During our 12 years of service, Paul on staff and me volunteering, our efforts were constantly rewarded by the interest displayed in the faces and questions of park visitors.

I really enjoyed working at the Lava Lands Visitor Center selling books and gifts in the bookshop,

and answering questions about "How far to.........?" or "Where can I get something to eat?" Many just wanted to learn what their options were for the day, and one lady asked "Why am I here?" I usually listed all there was to see and then suggested they start with the Interpretive Displays and choose what interested them most in the time they had to spend exploring. In summer, sometimes I gave a talk on identifying wildflowers.

7

Preface

The Newberry National Volcanic Monument is a fascinating place. I know because while my husband, Paul, was on the Forest Service staff there, I volunteered two half-days a week, mid-March through October, each summer at Lava Lands Visitor Center. The Center is twelve miles south of Bend, OR, on Highway 97. We did this for eight summers from 1991 through 1998, *when it was an exciting brand new monument.*

Then in 1999, Paul was assigned to do all the Interpretive Programs up inside the Newberry Caldera. Due to the higher elevation, the season at 6300 feet was only three months each summer. Paul still worked out of Lava Lands Visitor Center, but if I could be a full time volunteer, we could have the use of the old Forest Service Guard Station Bunkhouse. We fondly called it *the cabin*. So, we summered and worked out of the cabin across the road from Paulina Lake. The focus of Paul's demonstrations was the Geology and Archaeology of the area. At the Big Obsidian Flow he made stone tools, spears and atlatls. Obsidian was very valuable to Early Oregonians. My main focus was Anthropology, to explain what the evidence tells us of human occupation in the Newberry Caldera. I tried to help Monument visitors think about what life would have been like for these Semi-Nomadic Early Oregonians.

What would it be like to be summering up in the Newberry Caldera 9500 years ago? That was before the Bronze Age, the Iron age, the Egyptian pyramids, the Roman Empire, Stonehenge, Crater Lake, and before there were two lakes in Newberry Caldera. My intent is to give you a realistic idea of how it was, particularly from a woman's point of view.

Newberry Volcano

First, let's talk about the area where Newberry Volcano sits a little over twenty miles due south of Bend, Oregon. It is a **shield volcano** meaning that it spreads out with gently sloping sides like a warrior's shield lying on the ground instead

Looking almost due south from Pilot Butte Scenic Viewpoint in the middle of Bend, Newberry Volcano is a long low plateau on the horizon.

of building a cone shaped mountain. It's flattened because it spews fast-flowing, basaltic lava that spreads out into extensive horizontal layers, over and over again. The city of Bend sits on these layers with only about twelve inches of topsoil over a thick bed of lava. The area also includes over four-hundred smaller cone-shaped volcanic vents, or little mini volcanos, scattered on and around the main volcano. In fact, Pilot Butte, right in the middle of Bend, is one of these volcanic vents.

To look at Newberry Volcano from Bend, it is just a high uneven plateau with little indication that it's a volcano. Yet, this is the shape of the volcano and within it lies a seventeen square mile caldera, itself containing two pristine Alpine lakes. The caldera is the center of a five hundred square mile volcano, a volcano that remains both seismically and geothermally active to this day. It is a powerful source of energy that is in the process of being developed by private enterprise.

Newberry is an especially large volcano with two major fault zones crossing underneath. There have been many eruptions over the centuries, the last a mere 1,300 years ago.

Newberry National Volcanic Monument has over 50,000 acres of new and old basalt lava flows, rivers and streams, lakes and water falls, and many other spectacular geologic features. The highest point on the caldera rim is the summit of Paulina Peak at 7,985 feet. Find the peak in the picture below. This is where you will be if you drive to the top and where we went every morning to give our 10 AM talks. This view is backwards to the way it will look from the peak but this does give you a bigger view of the caldera floor.

You can see from this view why there is so much room for all the boating, fishing, campgrounds and trails.

Within the borders of the park, you will find boat docks, many miles of hiking trails, mountain bike trails, and horse trails. Up to date information should always be obtained from

This is the view you will see from the peak, with Paulina Lake on your left, East Lake on your right. The lake is divided by the Central Pumice Cone, Little Crater, and the boomerang shape is an older obsidian flow. The Big Obsidian Flow is central right just below Paulina Peak.

Lava Lands Visitor Center before going out on the trails.

The caldera itself is about five miles long and four miles wide and contains seven Forest Service camps including a horse camp, a group camp, two private resorts, and one private RV park. The road up to the caldera is plowed in winter as far as 10-Mile Snow Park, and you can snowmobile on up. But the volcano wasn't always a Monument. That didn't happen until 1990. After repeated efforts by many in Bend and across Oregon, the 101st Congress finally voted to approve the bill designating the Newberry National Volcanic Monument.

Lava Lands Visitor Center should always be your first stop. There you can pay your fee and will be given a guide called **The Volcanic Vista**. Open to the public from mid April until mid

Lava Lands Visitor Center, Bend, Oregon.

October every summer, the center is the hub for the Newberry National Volcanic Monument.

If you are intending to hike, bike, or go horseback riding, be sure to take water and let someone know where you are going. Some trails are remote and far from any help. Study the beautiful 3D topographical map of the entire park at the Lava Lands Visitor Center. Always know where you are. Cell phones may not work well inside the caldera walls.

Take time to walk through the Lawrence A. Chitwood Memorial Hall inside the Visitor Center. It will explain the complex geology that has made Lava Lands and the Newberry Volcano. The more you learn, the better you will enjoy your adventure. Near Lava Lands Visitor Center are trails that provide visitors with a chance to walk through some of the molten land, or walk the cooler shade of the whispering pines. Those two trails are wheelchair accessible. At the top of Lava Butte, you can also hike the crater rim as well.

Besides Lava Butte (1), there are several other points of

Lava Butte aerial image courtesy of Leading Edge Aviation, Bend, Oregon.

http://www.leadingedgeavn.com/

This is the Fire Watch building on top of Lava Butte. The public can't go up into the upper lookout, but they are encouraged to visit the lower floor where there is a 360 degree mural that names the surrounding mountains and landmarks. It is also a sheltered place to view the landscape on a cold or windy day.

interest that every visitor should see. Referring to the numbers on the USGS Park Map; (2) The Lava River Cave is the longest lava tube in Oregon at over a mile. (3) Benham Falls day use and picnic area on the Deschutes River is nice and there is a hike on to the falls. (4) The Lava Cast Forest is nine miles down an unimproved road.

Other points of interest are all in the caldera itself. Twelve miles south of the Lava Lands Visitor Center along Highway 97 is Paulina Lake Road. Take it another twelve miles east towards the volcano. (5) Don't miss Paulina Falls on your way in. They

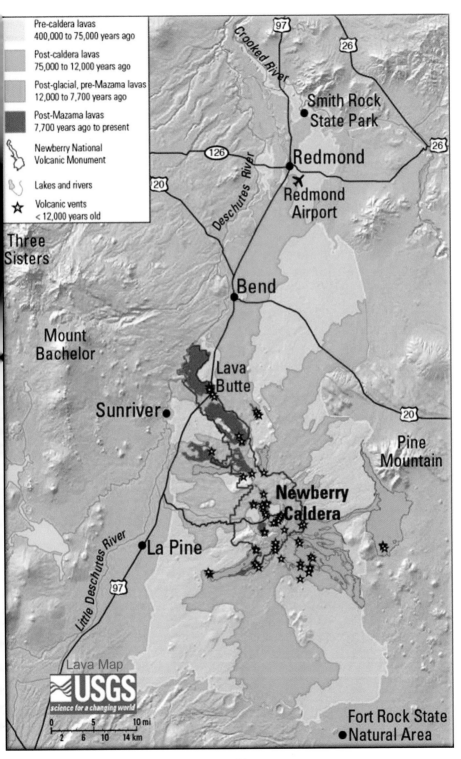

Pre-caldera lavas
400,000 to 75,000 years ago

Post-caldera lavas
75,000 to 12,000 years ago

Post-glacial, pre-Mazama lavas
12,000 to 7,700 years ago

Post-Mazama lavas
7,700 years ago to present

Newberry National
Volcanic Monument

Lakes and rivers

Volcanic vents
< 12,000 years old

Three Sisters

Mount Bachelor

Sunriver

La Pine

Smith Rock State Park

Redmond

Redmond Airport

Bend

Lava Butte

Newberry Caldera

Pine Mountain

Fort Rock State Natural Area

Crooked River

Deschutes River

Little Deschutes River

97

26

26

126

20

20

97

Lava Map

USGS
science for a changing world

0   5   10 mi
2   6   10   14 km

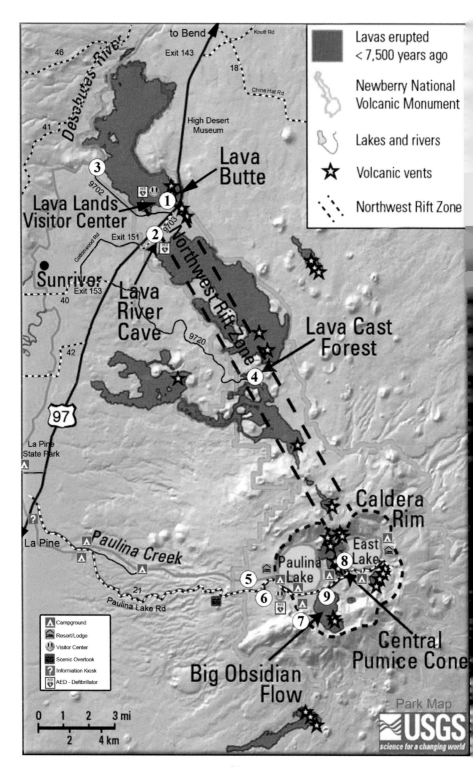

Lavas erupted
< 7,500 years ago

Newberry National
Volcanic Monument

Lakes and rivers

★ Volcanic vents

Northwest Rift Zone

to Bend
Knott Rd
Exit 143
18
China Hat Rd

46
Deschutes River
41
High Desert Museum

Lava Butte
③
①
Lava Lands Visitor Center
9702
9708
Northwest Rift Zone
Exit 151
②
Cottonwood Rd
Sunriver
Exit 153
40
Lava River Cave
42
9720
Lava Cast Forest
④

US 97

La Pine State Park

Caldera Rim

La Pine
Paulina Creek
⑤
Paulina Lake
East Lake
⑧
⑥
⑨
Paulina Lake Rd
21
⑦
Big Obsidian Flow
Central Pumice Cone

Campground
Resort/Lodge
Visitor Center
Scenic Overlook
Information Kiosk
AED - Defibrillator

0 1 2 3 mi
2 4 km

Park Map
USGS
science for a changing world

East Lake with people out fishing, and Central Pumice cone

Paulina Lake Campground - The lake can be seen through the trees.

drop nearly eighty feet over a volcanic cliff. (6) Stop in at the Paulina Visitor Center to see what the rangers have scheduled. (7) Paulina Peak opens in June or July depending upon weather, and is a must as the view from 8,000 feet can take your breath away. (8) The volcano's Central Cone also has an access trail that will take you up its flank. (9) The Big Obsidian Flow is the youngest lava flow in the park at only 1300 years old. Be sure to take the Big Obsidian Flow trail up on the edge of the flow. This is a must for first time visitors.

Newberry National Volcanic Monument is a picturesque area to spend a vacation exploring all the different sites. The campgrounds are well kept, the roads are good and the Forest Service personnel are there to help you. Usually, each campground has a host on site.

Introducing Mt. Mazama and Crater Lake

The western states have a whole row of mountains called the Cascades that have formed along a subduction zone, the shifting of the continental plates. These Cascades range from Mt. Lassen in Northern California up through Oregon and Washington, ending up at Mt. Garibaldi near Vancouver, British Columbia, Canada. They are all volcanos.

Most geologists think that Mt. Mazama was once a very large mountain like Mt. Shasta in northern California, maybe eleven to twelve thousand feet tall. It may have started building about four hundred thousand years ago. It erupted over and over in various vents along its sides forming an irregular shield volcano (Strato-volcano.) Then it went dormant for awhile. It became active again about 10,000 years ago. For several years it puffed and spewed steam, ash, lava and pumice from its many vents.

Finally, about 7700 years ago, all that action opened up the plug that was holding back the pressure, causing Mt. Mazama to explode in one huge eruption that sent hot steam, pumice and ash into the air that blanketed most of the northwestern states.

Ellen Morris Bishop, who wrote *In Search of Ancient Oregon, a Geological and Natural History*, states on page 235, that Mt. Mazama blasted first through a single vent like Mt. St. Helens. Then she describes the main huge eruption as a blast from one vent that "propelled an ash column tens of thousands of feet into the atmosphere, laden with rocks three feet in diameter. It left deposits seventy feet thick on the slopes of the mountain..... one half inch thick as far away as southwestern Saskatchewan." You would enjoy her book as she has the most beautiful landscape pictures you could want.

Having lost its base, the mountain collapsed down inside itself to form a caldera which collected rain and snow melt. The lake water measures nearly two thousand feet deep. Above the water, the cliffs rise another two thousand feet. This is the caldera that holds Crater Lake. Geologists tell us that **the eruption of Mt. Mazama was forty two times larger than the 1980 eruption of Mt. St. Helens**, and changed the face of southeast Oregon. At the same time, large thick layers of lava spewed from Mt. Mazama's many vents around the sides.

According to Bishop, the ash moved perhaps 100 mph with temperatures 1800° F (980° C). If you want to see some of this ash from Mt. Mazama, drive along Hwy 138, west from Diamond Lake after Toketee Falls. Look up at road cuts and you can see about 50 or 60 feet of ash dotted with spots of black charcoal from the trees that were burned or charred in the hot ash that fell from Mt. Mazama eruption.

Bishop also speaks about Mt. Mazama containing five sizeable strato-volcanos (shield) clustered together into a massive mountain that included Mt. Scott and Phantom Cone.

Geology of Oregon, Fourth Edition by Elizabeth L. Orr, William N. Orr, and Ewart M. Baldwin is a great book with

wonderful illustrations. On page 188, they speak of the study of sedimentation rates as the ash washed down the streams into the Columbia River and out to sea. "The distinctive Crater Lake ash and pumice layer ....is easily recognized in the deep marine environment off Oregon and provides a useful milepost for estimating rates of sedimentation."

Another note that I will mention here is the fact that most of the lake beds show layers of pumice and ash from Mt. Mazama but Diamond Lake has only a small amount. Some geologists believe that this is firm proof that Mt. Mazama erupted in winter, because Diamond Lake freezes over completely in winter. It would have been filled with ash, being so close to Crater Lake.

But the force of the explosion was so great, that the ash scooted across the ice like a hockey puck. Today, Diamond Lake is a popular recreation spot, noted for excellent fishing and boating.

Crater Lake is a wonderful shade of blue. I always thought this was a reflection of the sky, but we've been there when the lake was surrounded by snow under an overcast sky, and the water is still a deep blue! To my surprise, I learned that the beautiful color is from the purity of the water combined with the almost 2000 foot depth. Lets hope it always stays like this.

Crater Lake National Park was established in 1902 becoming America's fifth oldest, and Oregon's only, National Park. It is the deepest lake in Oregon, and one of the deepest in the world. It is also the image used on Oregon's memorial quarter. People come from near and far to see it. It is indeed a very special place.

When Crater Lake was being considered as a national park, Newberry Caldera was also in the competition. Long after Crater Lake had been chosen, efforts continued to give the Newberry Caldera some protection. Almost ninety years later that finally happened with the establishment of the Newberry National Volcanic Monument.

Both have had a great impact on our area in geological terms. The Mt. Mazama eruption devastated the Newberry area by depositing up to three feet of ash across the caldera floor thereby preserving the history of the plants, animals and people who lived there at the time.

One other interesting thing about Crater Lake is that the lake stays at about the same level because the losses due to evaporation and underground seepage balance with the inflow from rain and snow. Yearly snowfall within the caldera is measured in the hundreds of inches, and it can get very cold so dress warm if you visit during winter.

Opening the Book on Early Oregonians

When Newberry National Volcanic Monument was created in 1990, the first thing they needed was a better road up the volcano and into the caldera from Highway 97. This

This is a photo that I took in 1991 near the Paulina Visitor Center, where archaeologists were just starting a dig. In the hole you can see the layers of ash. They went deep enough to find the firepit and remains of a dwelling under the ash from Mt. Mazama and later eruptions within Newberry.

new monument was now being advertised internationally and tourists started coming from all over the world. However, before building roads or disturbing the soil, archaeological digs were required by law to collect and preserve the historical heritage. In fact, the widening and realignment of the Paulina-East Lake

Highway, located within the caldera itself, mandated a series of digs. The road from 97 up into the Caldera (Road 21) was also widened and redone.

This is Dr. Thomas Connolly, archaeologist for the University of Oregon who supervised the digs in 1991 and 1992, and author of the book about the findings which came out in 1999.

I include the photo above taken of a display at the Lava Lands Visitor Center to help you think about the layers of ash that was covering the fire pit and wickiup found in the dig. Plan to spend plenty of time reviewing the information available. There are many displays about the complicated geology and archaeology of the area.

One of my favorite displays is about the underwater exploration on Paulina Lake because archaeologists were scuba diving while we were there. The Lava Lands Visitor Center also has a book and gift shop besides the interpretive displays.

A dig starts out by staking off a square meter on the selected area. Every bit of soil inside this perimeter is removed down several feet and put through a screen. The items found during screening are labeled with where and at what depth they were found, and preserved for later study. In productive sites, the dig is widened and deepened.

In all, nine dig sites were developed in 1991, and four more the following year. All this digging produced many artifacts, but one dig, near Paulina Lake, came right down on an ancient fire pit. Three other sites proved to be especially fruitful as well. What was found in these four sites was summarized in a book by the supervisor of the digs, Thomas Connolly, and published in 1999 titled: *NEWBERRY CRATER - A Ten-Thousand Year Record of Human Occupation and Environmental Change in the Basin Plateau Borderlands*.

Every dig had to go below a layer of ash laid down by Mount Mazama when it erupted to form Crater Lake 7700 years ago. Nearly three feet of ash was deposited in the caldera from seventy-five miles away. The ash was thicker closer to the eruption. Mount Mazama covered the land with a thick blanket of hot smoking ash. It devastated the land in the caldera and a lot of central Oregon. We do not know what became of the people who lived there so long ago. Their summer camp was covered, and also the sage brush bark sandals in Fort Rock cave to the East in Central Oregon where these people may have spent their winters. Evidence seems to show them to be the same people who occupied both sites.

The dig at Paulina went below the ash from Mazama and turned up evidence of the people who summered there 9500 years ago. Archaeologists found the charred remains of posts set deeply into the ground on an inward slant so that they could be joined at the top. Large stones were arranged in an oblong shape indicating what Native American's call a wickiup, or house. A wickiup is made to be permanent whereas a tepee is light and small and can be carried from camp to camp. The larger stones were arranged in an oval which defined a space seventeen by thirteen feet. The walls probably consisted of reed mats held down by these stones along the outside of the house.

The fire pit inside the wickiup was recessed a foot or more and contained bits of lodgepole and ponderosa pine carbondated to 9500 years ago. Analyzing plant fibers and pollens found inside the structure indicated it was a damper climate back then, more like the Willamette Valley is today. There were lomatium, camas, rice root lily, filbert trees, salmonberry, blackberry, buckwheat, herbs, and chokecherrys.

Many non-obsidian tools were found including abraders, heavy mauls, edge faceted cobbles, cobble spall knives, and chopper tools. The cobbles are round smooth river rocks, used for many things including dropping hot rocks into a basket of water to heat a broth or medicinal tea. The spear points were obsidian in the stemmed or willow leaf styles

Stains on some of these spear points were found to be long-dried protein from the blood of elk, deer, bison, bear, sheep, and rabbits. It is interesting that no human blood was found on any of the points. Anthropologists concluded that these early Oregonians were there to hunt and dry meat, and to gather bulbs, seeds, nuts and herbs, more than to collect the obsidian that was there at that time.

Winters are severe at 6300 feet, so it is reasonable to assume they would have wintered at lower elevations. The Fort Rock Caves would have been a good choice. They could get fresh fish from the lake throughout the winter. Evidence of these people have been discovered in many caves throughout Oregon.

When the wickiup was carbon dated at 9500 years ago, it instantly became the *oldest man-made dwelling* ever found in Oregon as of this writing. Older *found-in-nature dwellings*, such as caves, overhangs and other rock shelters have been found.

One of the most famous and oldest found in nature dwellings is the Preclovis site called *Meadowcroft Rockshelter* on the bank of Cross Creek, a tributary of the Ohio River in Pennsylvania, USA. It has been dated at 14,000 years. Data suggests they were also hunters and gatherers.

In Oregon, we have the Paisley caves in the Summer Lake Basin, also known as the *Paisley Five-Mile Caves* near Paisley Oregon, a group of eight caves and rockshelters in Lake County. Evidence there has been found of human DNA as far back as 14,300 BP and obsidian spear points that date 13,200 years old. There are many caves in Oregon that add to our knowledge.

There were many lakes as the Ice Age ended where water levels and their wave action created a lot of caves and overhangs, called rockshelters. Those are all called *found in nature* dwellings. We have a long and complicated past, and trying to read the evidence is an exciting study. Early Americans have been around for a long, long time.

The scientists added another piece of the prehistorical puzzle when the carbon-dates on the Paulina Lake Site turned out to be contemporary with over a hundred pairs of sage brush bark sandals that were previously found in Fort Rock Cave. This is important because it is believed it was the same group of people who camped in summer at Paulina Lake and who traveled to lower elevations at Fort Rock Cave for the winter months. I will speak more about the sandals later.

The Paulina Lake wickiup is also contemporary with Kennewick Man whose remains were found in the mud along the Columbia River near Kennewick, Washington State, and carbon-dated to 9000 years old. He could have interacted with the early Oregonians here at Paulina Lake before continuing a journey that ended abruptly with his death.

However, the features of Kennewick Man do not resemble those of the Native Americans in this area today. They are more like the Ancient Ainu of Northern Japan. The area was not much occupied after the Mt. Mazama ash, except to collect obsidian. The Northern Piautes moved in many years later, and assumed the semi-nomadic life style required to live in the now much dryer high desert country of central Oregon.

The story of Kennewick Man is ongoing as many Native American tribes have petitioned to be given the remains so that they can rebury him and allow him to continue his journey in peace into the next world. They believe he cannot rest in peace until he is buried while scientists want to study him to see what his remains can reveal. Was this a tribe forever lost to us?

Living Native Americans also contributed to what we know. Their stories passed down for thousands of years are recorded in a book entitled **The First Oregonians**, *An Illustrated Collection of Essays on Traditional Lifeways, Federal-Indian Relations, and the State's Native People Today* published by the Oregon Council for the Humanities in 1991. This book contains word-of-mouth histories from modern native Oregonians who have grown up listening to the stories of their ancestors and recorded them so that they would not be lost. The illustrations in this book are wonderful and helped me understand how people lived 9500 years ago. This is in fact, my favorite of all the references I used. I recommend it.

The stories told of constant seasonal migrations as they went where the food was ripe and available to harvest. These people would have traveled over a large part of Central Oregon during a summer season. But, they would have returned to lower elevations along a river or lake to spend the winters surviving on fish, birds, and plants near the water's edge.

There is little doubt that life was physically hard being a woman back then. They were responsible for gathering and processing plants, drying the meat the men brought in, the cooking, tanning leather, making clothing, blankets, baskets, shoes, tending the sick or elderly, and child rearing. They moved a lot and had no other way to carry their belongings except on their backs. It was a perpetual camping trip.

The **High Desert Museum** is another great place to learn about the Native Americans in this area. It is about seven miles south of Bend on Highway 97. Plan to spend a whole day there. I very highly recommend it. We took our grandsons often when they were young. The museum taught them about the First Oregonians as well as the ever-changing ecology of Oregon's high desert. They learned that the first white people to come west were the fur trappers, traders and surveyors, long before the covered wagons came filled with miners, loggers, ranchers, shop-owners, and others that settled the area around Bend.

The High Country

The Newberry area is popular in winter for Nordic activities. It is great for snow-shoeing, sledding, cross-country sking and snowmobiling. The lakes are frozen over in winter and the snow is deep. The road from Highway 97 up to Newberry is plowed as far as "Ten-Mile SnowPark". You can go for the day just to play in the snow, or park and snowmobile up into the caldera. Paulina Resort closes after the tourist season for a

while, and they take a second break in the spring, opening up when fishing season starts. It's best to get up to date information on cabins for rent and if meals are served. The weather is always a big factor.

Newberry Caldera is much higher elevation (6300 feet) and thus, campgrounds are only open three months each summer. We usually got our first light snows in August. Paul and I were to do all the Interpretive Programs within the caldera, and if I could be a full-time volunteer, we could have the use of the Guard Station Bunkhouse which we fondly called *the Cabin*.

It was June 9, 1999, our 44th wedding anniversary, when we arrived at the cabin near Paulina Lake. We pulled our RV into the driveway as far as it could go, and looked out on hip deep snow blocking the front door. So, we went around to the back entrance which was sheltered by a firewood shed. Besides firewood, inside the shed was an axe and chopping block, and

tools for shoveling snow, all of which would come in handy later that day. We entered, walked through the cabin, and opened the front door. At least three feet of snow blocked the exit. And this was just the remains of what had accumulated over the winter. Sometimes it didn't all melt until into July.

We immediately fired up the old wood stove and were busy cleaning when we heard the loud rumble of an engine break the stillness. It was the park manager coming down the hill towards the cabin with a backhoe. He made short work of the snow right up to our front door in minutes.

Just a few yards from our cabin, the park manager and his wife were working in the old Guard Station setting up an information center and gift shop. Then, to our surprise, we soon heard the backhoe again. Yes, it was the park manager coming back but this time hauling a couch, a matching chair, and a large work table. He delivered them right to our front door in the scoop. We learned early that summer that the manager had a special relationship with heavy equipment. The memory of that fine spring morning still makes me smile. I wish I had a picture of him making his delivery.

That was the best of times. That summer, Paul and I did three programs a day plus two evening programs on week-ends. Monday and Tuesday we were off to do our laundry and a trip to town for our groceries and supplies for home and work. We were always very busy. We made all the arrangements for guest speakers, published the bulletins, filled out the reports, and promoted our programs when we had time. We set our own schedule to allow at least thirty minutes between programs to relax in the cabin. Our age was slowing us down.

The park manager and his wife, who ran the Gift Shop and Information Center, were very special to us. We had great times together solving problems and helping each other. It was such fun working with them.

Best of all, working in Newberry was another job we could do together which meant a lot to me. Most of our married life, we did our separate jobs, both too busy. This job allowed us to share the experiences and challenges of each new day together. What a wonderful way to fully enjoy our retirement.

Flintknapping

The people who lived here *before the ash fell* were expert tool makers. There have been lots of their obsidian tools and points found during the digs.

The term flintknapping was used to describe the shaping of flint for the old flint-lock rifles, but now the term is used for the shaping of tools made from any stone. Today this is mostly a lost art, but 9500 years ago, it meant life or death.

Paul had been flintknapping for about ten years and was very good at it. To make his spear points, he used cobble stones for shaping and deer antler for pressure flaking just as the early tool makers would have done. Most tourists really enjoyed watching him work the obsidian. After making a point, he would present it to a tourist, so his points are now spread across the US and in many other countries. He presented it with a card saying it was made from Glass Butte Obsidian that was five million years old. Glass Butte is about halfway between Bend and Burns, Oregon, on Highway 20. It is a very old mountain and has really good grade obsidian. It is BLM land and open to the public. It is

Paul's work was so much appreciated that his name was added to the Program area sign in 2002 before we retired.

Hot Topics!
11:30am & 2pm, Thurs. – Sunday

Join a Ranger at the Big Obsidian Flow amphitheater for a 20 minute Ranger talk. Topics vary; from wildlife to geology to human history. Meet the Ranger at Paul's Place amphitheater in the Big Obsidian Flow day use site.

illegal to take any objects from Newberry.

We were very surprised when we visited the Newberry Caldera again in 2013 that his name is still there and that the current Interpreter has said "meet the Ranger at Paul's Place" for a program. I expect Paul had demonstrated his program on Flintknapping, spears and atlatls hundred of times in that Amphitheater or at a picnic table near Big Obsidian Flow trail. Paul always has given more than 100% with his usual wit and good humor. He is always eager to help. I am glad he was appreciated and we always had great fun.

Obsidian is volcanic glass and all glass breaks with a conchoidal fracture, a concept central to stone tool making. It fractures to an edge sharper than a steel blade. Therefore, precautions must be taken to keep from getting badly cut. I do not recommend trying this at home. Obsidian blades have been used in modern eye surgery.

Paul and I always took special care to explain, especially to the children in our audiences, that *artifacts* were items that were really old, and had been used by people a long time ago, whereas *replicas* are modern copies made to look like the real thing. It is an important distinction. Paul became very skilled at making replicas. His display board shows the replicas that he made.

Our 9x5 inch biface was also called a *hunters tool box* because it is a large stone, pre-shaped to allow other smaller chips to be taken from it for spear points, blades or other tools when needed. Sometimes several of these have been found cached for later trading or tool making.

Each volcanic flow has a particular mineral fingerprint and can be traced to its source. Newberry obsidian has been traced all over the Northwest particularly to the North.

My husband demonstrated what is usually considered **man's work** of preparing tools for the hunt. I wanted to make my own display at a nearby table to demonstrate what is usually considered **woman's work**. I wanted to share what the evidence reveals about life some 9500 years ago, as shown by artifacts from the Newberry Archaeological dig and others throughout Central Oregon. We prepared formal presentations to large groups, and the visual aids we created allowed us to just chat with visitors about what life was like back then.

When I put my display together, I decided it needed a sign big enough to get everyone's attention. I made a large tri-fold backboard and used large stick-on letters for the main heading, **9500** YEARS AGO, EARLY AMERICANS LIVED HERE. If tourists remembered only one thing from my display, they should remember *that*, even if only seen from the trail as they walked by. The backboard changed and evolved over the years beginning with my laminating as much of the display as possible to make it waterproof. I also added a few animal pelts as table coverings and reed mats to show how these industrious people used their natural resources to make clothing and other necessities.

Newberry is high enough that it creates its own weather pattern, often not friendly. Summer at 6300 feet included frequent lightning storms with afternoon showers or hail that could strike in minutes. To combat this, we bought large, light-weight, see-through plastic drop cloths to go over our displays. If there were only a few raindrops, we would continue our talk. However, if the clouds indicated a heavy rain, we could pack things up pretty fast, and retreat to the cabin. This happened often during our evening slide shows. Getting rained out was normal.

I made some sample pemmican from pieces of dried meat, dried cranberries and cherries, seeds and nuts: the first trail mix. I tried to make samples of something similar to what the early Oregonians might have had. I made sure that the squirrels stayed out of the pemmican, dried camas bulbs, baskets of seeds, and other dried foods by clustering them at the end of the table where I stood. I left some nuts within their reach and the children loved it when these playful and inquisitive animals snatched a filbert. Both chipmunks and squirrels have cheek pouches, and they

would stuff their cheeks so full that they puffed way out to the delight of many. The small ones with stripes on their faces are Yellow-Pine Chipmunks. The other ones are Golden-Mantled Ground Squirrels. They were doing their hunting and gathering for the long winter and I was an easy target. During hibernation, they wake occasionally to eat from their stash.

I have mentioned several times about the Fort Rock Caves, and the Sage Brush Bark Sandals that have been found in digs there. A great little book called **The Sandal and the Cave**, by Luther Cressman, Department of Anthropology, University of Oregon, Eugene, came out in 1981. Dr. Cressman supervised a dig in 1938 that uncovered Sage Brush Bark Sandals which were carbon-dated to around 9000 years old. That gave archaeologists a clue that people had occupied Oregon much earlier than thought before. Additional digs in central Oregon caves and rockshelters have yielded over 100 pair of sandals. You might see a pair on display at the High Desert Museum about six miles south of Bend on Hwy 97. These left/right images of a typical pair of sandals are courtesy of the University of Oregon's Museum of Natural and Cultural History.

Sage Brush Bark Sandals were made by taking long strips of bark and twisting them into a cord and then twisting back again on itself to make a rope about the size of your little finger. These were tied together with plant fibers to make a sole with a heavy tread. A cap came over the toes. Since mud from Fort Rock Lake was embedded into the fibers of sandals that had been worn, it seems these fiber sandals were worn around the slippery shores of the lake, and on the ice and snows of their winter times near the lakes or rivers, where they could survive on fish and water plants. Rabbit skins could have been wrapped around the feet inside the sandals for warmth in winter. No sandals were found in Newberry.

The reason these plant fiber items lasted so long is amazing, and due to the ash of Mt. Mazama that sifted down around the fibers sealing them off from the weather. Those Sage Brush Bark Sandals were preserved at the same time that the ash covered the remains of the wickiup in Newberry. But, why so many? Maybe they were made as trade items on trips to the North. Why abandoned? Did they leave quickly due to some danger. Or did they not get back to the caves for winter. Some questions have not been answered for us yet. This book is about the history buried under the ash from Mt. Mazama that formed Crater Lake about 7700 Years ago.

COOKING POT
BASKETS WERE TIGHTLY WOVEN
SEALED WITH PINE PITCH AND
LIQUID WAS HEATED BY HOT
STONES FROM THE FIREPIT.
TONGS
WERE USED TO TRANSFER
THE STONES.

They had no pottery. They had baskets, skins and leather sacks. The baskets women used for gathering, storing and traveling were large utility baskets. Some were large, open-topped for gathering nuts and digging roots with a digging stick. They were large and slung on their backs. I decided to buy dolls, dress them in furs and leathers, and make baskets to scale to demonstrate how they would have been used.

The basket I purchased to demonstrate a cooking pot was not as tightly woven as the early Oregonians would have made it, but it served its purpose for my display. Paul made a pair of tongs from willow bark. The tongs were made from green willow bark freshly stripped off a limb, bent and tied together at the ends. After it had dried for a short while, the bark was still springy enough to make good tongs and strong enough to grasp rocks and drop them into the cooking pot for a broth or medicinal tea.

Doll One has the wide cone-shaped, tightly-woven basket and carries a stick with which she hits plants with small seeds and lets them fall into the basket. She also has a small pouch over her shoulder for gathering plant fibers such as sage brush bark.

Doll Two has the large round basket they used for carrying a load from place to place. The weight of the basket and whatever's in it hangs from the band around her head. Additional control was made using strings which she can either tie around her waist or hold them in her hands to keep the load from shifting.

Doll Three has a digging stick and a large basket that extended high on her back with a gaping opening. It too hung from a band around her head. This freed her hands to dig for roots or pick berries which would then be tossed into the basket. She would have dug camas, rice root lilies, or any number of other tubers and roots, maybe even mushrooms. I later wove sandals for my dolls from jute string to resemble the Sage Brush Bark Sandals found at Fort Rock Cave.

For all their baskets, I followed the examples found in the book entitled *The First Oregonians*, listed in my bibliography. If you are interested in further study, I suggest you get a copy. It has great illustrations.

Finally, I couldn't resist making a cradle-board with a baby. Caring for the infants, toddlers and young fell to the women and those unable to gather or hunt.

We always received a generous response from those who listened to our talks and looked at our displays. I think my items on display served its purpose to help people think about life so long ago. It gave them a visual idea of long ago living.

9500 YEARS AGO
EARLY AMERICANS
LIVED HERE

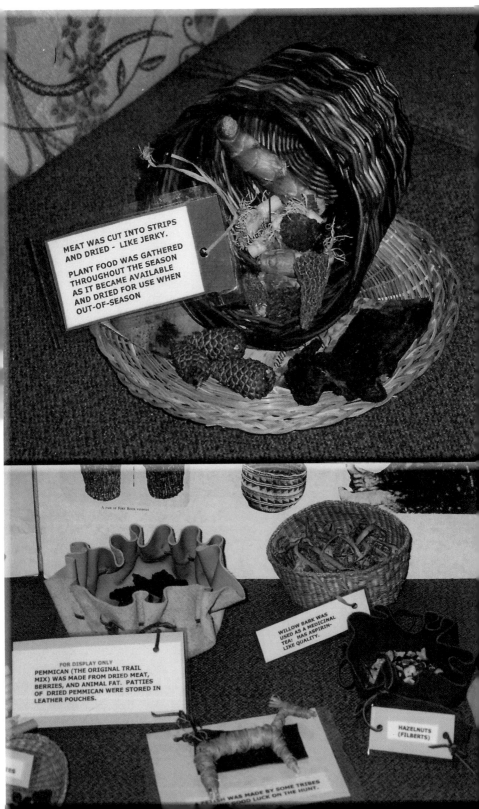

MEAT WAS CUT INTO STRIPS
AND DRIED - LIKE JERKY.

PLANT FOOD WAS GATHERED
THROUGHOUT THE SEASON
AS IT BECAME AVAILABLE
AND DRIED FOR USE WHEN
OUT-OF-SEASON

A PAIR OF FORT ROCK SANDALS

FOR DISPLAY ONLY
PEMMICAN (THE ORIGINAL TRAIL
MIX) WAS MADE FROM DRIED MEAT,
BERRIES, AND ANIMAL FAT. PATTIES
OF DRIED PEMMICAN WERE STORED IN
LEATHER POUCHES.

WILLOW BARK WAS
USED AS A MEDICINAL
TEA: HAS ASPIRIN-
LIKE QUALITY.

HAZELNUTS
(FILBERTS)

...ASH WAS MADE BY SOME TRIBES
...GOOD LUCK ON THE HUNT.

A Day In The Life

Paul and I spent a lot of time walking the same trails as the people who lived here 9500 years ago. We couldn't help but wonder at how they spent their time. Perhaps a never ending camping trip might sound like fun right now, their lives were hard and short and all about survival. A day in the life of a woman 9500 years ago might have gone something like this:

Morning

Even in the heart of summer, a large cooking fire would be welcome first thing in the morning at that elevation of 6300 ft. It gets very cold every night. They would need fur blankets to sleep in for comfort. We can assume that when these Early Oregonians got up from the bed, had gone to the lake to wash up, they would want something to eat. They worked hard and expended a lot of energy which requires calories. Women, being the main care-givers in most societies, had to give special care to the ill, the old, the small children and take care of any special morning needs of others. So, there was probably something hot prepared to start the day.

Using a rock mortar and a stone pestle, they crushed nuts, seeds, roots, spices and bits of meat into a coarse mixture which then moistened with a bit of water and pressed into a flattened ball. A few moments on the hot cooking stone provided them with a fine hot meal similar to a croquette or flat meatball. It could be eaten hot off the fire or saved for later. Cooking preserved the food which could be made into a hot stew or ground finer and made into flatbread, pancake or tortilla type bread. And there was always meat drying by a fire.

If the women did not have to "gather" that day, they might sit around the fire doing chores. As they did their chores, they watched the young children and told the stories of their ancestry. Girls who were old enough, were being taught crafts. Reeds could be used to weave floor mats, or repair a hole in the wickiup walls, or create the many baskets needed. They would have spent a lot of time preparing the leather to make clothing and moccasins, tanning and scraping the hides until supple. The making of clothing would have taken a lot of work, punching a row of holes with an obsidian awl, cutting the hide with a sharp obsidian blade. Children learned life skills as they worked with the adults, *the original home schooling*. Remnants of baskets and netting have been found deep in caves throughout Central Oregon recorded in C.Melvin Aikens book: **Archaeology of Oregon**, 1993, listed in the bibliography.

Midday

Meanwhile, the men must have spent long hours on their tools preparing for the next hunt: straightening wooden shafts for spears, making new spear points and sharpening old ones, and last but not least, making sure the spear points were firmly attached to the shaft with lacings and pine pitch. The men probably also worked on string for the making of nets to catch rabbits, ropes for tying, snares for trapping, firewood for the hearth, and teaching the young boys these skills.

If the women were out "gathering," the mid-day meal might be eaten under a tree and consist of pemmican, which is dried meats, nuts, fruits, berries and seeds. Think of pemmican as the *first trail mix*. Very nutritious, easy to carry.

Evening

Think of your own camping trips. No appointments, meetings and no schedule other than to do your fishing or hiking or napping or eating when hungry. I do not think these early Americans had meals at certain times as we do today. They might have waited until the sun was high above, to ward off mosquitoes, to go gathering or digging roots. They may have carried lunch just as we would do on a hike. I have noticed that even the wild animals take a quiet time to rest during the heat of the afternoon. People take siestas, so I would think that these Early Oregonians would have had a rest time at some point during the mid-day, whenever they needed. And they might have eaten a snack at rest time.

As the sun sank low in the west, the last meal of the day would have been taken before nightfall.

If the hunters had been successful, fresh rabbit or venison, cut into fine slices, would be roasting over the open fire. While the meat cooked, the animal's bones were broken open using

smooth round river rocks to get at the rich marrow.

The meal could include chokecherries, fresh greens, and filberts from the afternoon gatherings. I should mention that although these early Oregonians were also excellent fishermen, there were no fish in what was then just one big lake 9500 years ago. The lake's only source of water was rain and snowfall. Both lakes do have small hot springs that come up and mix with the lake water, but that is from seepage that is heated and comes back up. There are no streams feeding the lakes and the fish would not be able to negotiate Paulina Falls. However, crayfish made it past the waterfall into the caldera and may have been a welcome dietary addition. Only much later did the Oregon Fish and Game start stocking the lakes with fish. Today, there is wonderful fishing in Newberry so don't forget your fishing pole when you visit.

As the sun went down, the heat coming off the fire would draw the tribe closer. Extra furs would be brought out to wrap around shoulders, but I doubt they were up much after dark.

I expect there were masses of mosquitoes and other bugs 9500 years ago, just as there are today. The smoke from the fire, when we were there, was not enough to keep the mosquitoes at bay. When Paul and I summered at Paulina Lake, the mosquitoes seemed to be unusually big and hungry, especially after a fresh hatch from the shallow reed-filled areas at the lake edge. There were fewer at East Lake because the shore is white pumice and it gets more breeze.

Night

After every long summer day came a cold night. Putting away the food at night might not have been easy since bears are great climbers of trees. But we assume that they stored things inside the wickiup by hanging them in baskets. Outside, they might have kept a fire going and a watchmen to protect their drying meat. We do not know. I think rodents would have been their biggest problem. If the wild animals, such as bears, have an abundance of food, they avoid humans. It's when we move into their territory and they get hungry, that they come around. It was pretty secure inside their wickiup, wrapped in furs with rocks over the door flap.

I can just imagine the night sounds of water birds on the lake, owls in the trees, and the rustle of night critters at the water's edge.

Our Other Programs

My main program was the display showing the every day activities of the ancient Oregonians, especially the women. Paul's was his excellent flintknapping demonstration. However, these were not the only programs Paul and I put together.

Skulls

One of the popular talks Paul and I gave was on the reading of skulls. Animal skulls have evolved for millions of years to protect the brain and provide a stable platform for the sensory organs. Studying or reading a skull can reveal the animal's dietary and social patterns such as whether the animal was a herbivore, omnivore or carnivore. Carnivores generally have large eyes facing forward and the field of vision of the two eyes overlap giving the animal binocular sight with excellent depth perception.

On the other hand, herbivores have eyes that face to the side, giving them monocular vision. In other words, they see an object with only one eye at a time. While herbivores lack depth perception, they can watch for approaching predators in all directions. Some speedy herbivores, like deer, have eyes that overlap slightly. This provides limited depth perception so they don't run into trees as they flee from danger.

Omnivores have eyes facing mainly to the front with good overlap. This also gives them excellent binocular vision and helps in their search for a wide variety of prey.

A carnivore's teeth is used to tear meat, a herbivore's to chew plants. Just from examining the connection of the spine to the skull, you can determine if the animal walked on all fours or on two feet. Even intelligence can be estimated by the size of the brain cavity. For many children in our audience, this was the closest they had ever been to a skull. Our small collection fascinated boys and girls alike.

Red Crossbill

Cedar Waxwing

Rufous Hummingbird

Birds

Paul obtained a permit from Oregon Fish and Game to collect and preserve any dead birds found in the park. Many died

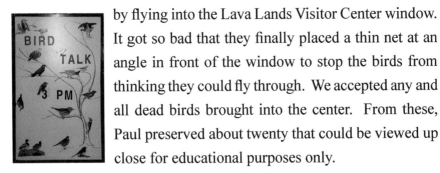

by flying into the Lava Lands Visitor Center window. It got so bad that they finally placed a thin net at an angle in front of the window to stop the birds from thinking they could fly through. We accepted any and all dead birds brought into the center. From these, Paul preserved about twenty that could be viewed up close for educational purposes only.

For instance, it was much easier to understand how a Red Crossbill can pry nuts from pine cones with his crossed beak if you could look at the bird and his strange beak. Any hummingbird seen up close is fascinating. They have long slender beaks, and an even longer tongue to lap nectar several times per second. One of my personal favorites is the Cedar Waxwing, so formally dressed and splendidly colored. The feathers on all the birds held their color and made a great study for park visitors.

Under the Microscope

Another popular talk involved looking in a microscope. We usually did this together so one of us could help people looking in the eyepiece and help keep the live creatures in focus. While waiting for their turn the kids looked at illustrations in one of our books. They also seemed to like viewing beetles, mosquitoes and butterfly wings under the scope. They were fascinated by the live, swimming cyclops, water fleas, rotifers, and other small critters found in stagnant, shallow water at the edge of Paulina Lake, or from Lost Lake, a small shallow catch-basin near the start of the Big Obsidian flow trail, where a family of Mallards hatched every summer.

Paulina Peak

Each morning, Paul and I would drive up the narrow road to the summit of Paulina Peak to give a talk and visit with tourists. At almost 8000 feet, Paulina Peak is the highest point in the caldera's rim. In the picture above, you can clearly see the rim, four miles away, across the caldera, and across Paulina Lake.

Paul and I would identify as many landmarks as it was clear enough to see. In the picture above, he is pointing out the Three Sisters, with Broken Top in front from this angle.

In the next picture, you can see just a bit of the Big Obsidian Flow down in the right corner, which is the youngest eruption happening only about 1300 years ago. Paul was very good

at relating the geology of the area, explaining volcanism and telling the history of the early Oregonians. You can also see how difficult life is for the few trees up there at almost 8000 ft. The winter winds are very strong and cold. In the photo above you can see a little line running through the trees on the caldera floor which is the Paulina East-Lake Road. The boomerang shape you see, left of the Central Pumice Cone, is an older Obsidian Flow.

We borrowed a topographical model of Newberry from the Forest Service and used it to explain the various landmarks and geology. The model opened up vertically and showed some of the many volcanic vents coming up from deep down in the earth. It was especially useful when the caldera was fogged in.

Slide Show

On those rare occasions when we didn't have a speaker lined up, Paul and I gave slide shows for our week-end evening programs. For that we had to have a generator for power after dark. We showed ***BIRDS OF OREGON, WILDFLOWERS OF OREGON, and SCENES OF OREGON*** introducing our state, and showing tourists other areas they might enjoy.

Paul is doing a flintknapping in Newberry

Paul is demonstrating spears and atlatls to a group of school children at Lava Lands Visitor Center

To Thompson
2619 SE Myrtle Wood Way
Gresham OR
97080-7261

Last Word

Our humble efforts were constantly rewarded by the interest displayed in the faces and questions of the park visitors. Many openly voiced their appreciation for our efforts. Some came back year after year.

Others followed us around to hear and participate in all our programs and talks. We often had Forest Service archaeologists, anthropologists, biologists and geologists do special programs for us. Even the professionals appreciated our work. Perhaps most of all, we received so much pleasure and enjoyment from our contact with the thousands of people visiting the Newberry National Volcanic Monument each year. It was a once in a lifetime opportunity made even better because I shared it with the man I love.

For years after we left, we heard that occasionally someone would still ask, *"Whatever happened to that nice old couple who did programs up here? I really enjoyed them."* It's nice to be missed and know we had made a difference.

Above is beautiful Paulina Falls spilling over the rim of the Newberry Caldera. It is the only outlet from the two lakes.

Evelyn Findley

Bibliography

Newberry Crater - A Ten-Thousand Year Record of Human Occupation and Environmental Change in the Basin Plateau Borderlands: by Thomas J. Connolly (with contributions by Dennis L. Jenkins et al); University of Utah Anthropological Papers, Number 121; Copyright 1999 by the University of Utah Press, Salt Lake City; ISBN 0874805740 / 978-0874805741

The First Oregonians - An Illustrated Collection of Essays on Traditional Lifeways, Federal-Indian Relations, and the State's Native People Today: Published by the Oregon Council for the Humanities. Edited by Carolyn M. Buan and Richard Lewis, Designed by Jeanne E. Galick. Copyright 1991 by the Oregon Council for the Humanities, Portland, Oregon; ISBN 1-880377-00-4; Library of Congress Catalog Card Number 92-6052.

Oregon, The Northwest Perspective: University of Oregon; Oregon Quarterly (Magazine), Summer 1999, (Pages 24-28). Copyright 1999 University of Oregon. Editor, Oregon Quarterly, 5228 University of Oregon Eugene, Oregon 97403-5228.

The Sandal and the Cave, The Indians of Oregon: by L.S. Cressman; Department of Anthropology, University of Oregon, printed by Oregon State University Press, Corvallis, Oregon. Copyright 1981 Luther S. Cressman, ISBN O-87O71-O78-8.

Newberry National Volcanic Monument: Expanded Edition by Stuart G. Garrett. an Oregon Documentary - Bert Webber, Editor, WEBB RESEARCH GROUP PUBLISHERS, P.O. Box 314, Medford, Oregon 97501. Copyright 1991 Stuart G. Garrett; ISBN 0-936738-46-4

Roadside Guide to the Geology of Newberry Volcano: by Robert A. Jensen; Copyright 1988, 1995, 2000 Printed by The Press Pros, Bend, Oregon; ISBN 0-9646287-1-6

Archaeology of Oregon: by C. Melvin Aikens; 1993, U.S. Department of the Interior, Bureau of Land Management, Oregon State Office, 1300 N. E. 44th Avenue, Portland, Oregon 97213

Newbery Crater: Paulina Lake Site (35DS34) http://www.oregon-archaeology.com/theory/housing/southeast/#newbery

In Search of Ancient Oregon, A geological and Natural History by Ellen Morris Bishop, copyright 2003, ISBN 0-88192-590-x .Timber Press, Inc., The Haseltine Building, 133 S.W. Second Ave, Suite 450, Portland, Oregon 97204 USA.

Geology of Oregon, Fourth Edition, by Elizabeth L. Orr, William N. Orr, and Ewart M. Baldwin, ISBN 0-8403-8058-5, copyright 1964 by Ewart M. Baldwin , copyright 1976, 1981, 1992 by Kendall/Hunt Publishing Company

Newberry artifacts span nearly 10,000 years, Jan 3,1993; http://news. google.com/newspapers?nid=1243&dat=19930103&id=C5ZTAAAAIBAJ &sjid=I4cDAAAAIBAJ&pg=6770,5390745

The Museum of Natural and Cultural History - University of Oregon: http://natural-history.uoregon.edu

WRITERS CRAMP PUBLISHING
http://www.writerscramp.us/